Thanksgiving
※ in the ※
White House

Gary Hines • Illustrated by Alexandra Wallner

Henry Holt and Company • New York

Henry Holt and Company, LLC
Publishers since 1866
115 West 18th Street
New York, New York 10011
www.henryholt.com

Henry Holt is a registered trademark
of Henry Holt and Company, LLC
Text copyright © 2003 by Gary Hines
Illustrations copyright © 2003 by Alexandra Wallner
All rights reserved.
Distributed in Canada by H. B. Fenn and Company Ltd.

Library of Congress Cataloging-in-Publication Data
Hines, Gary.
Thanksgiving in the White House / Gary Hines;
illustrated by Alexandra Wallner.
Summary: Young Tad Lincoln is excited about the new national holiday until
he learns that the cook plans to serve Jack the turkey as
the main course for Thanksgiving dinner.
1. Lincoln, Thomas, 1853–1871—Juvenile fiction.
2. Thanksgiving Day—History—Juvenile fiction.
3. Lincoln, Abraham, 1809–1865—Juvenile fiction.
[1. Lincoln, Thomas, 1853–1871—Juvenile fiction. 2. Thanksgiving Day—Fiction.
3. Turkeys—Fiction. 4. Lincoln, Abraham, 1809–1865—Fiction.
5. White House (Washington, D.C.)—Fiction.]
I. Wallner, Alexandra, ill. II. Title.
PZ7.H5715 Th 2002 [Fic]—dc21 2001002667

ISBN 0-8050-6530-X
First Edition—2003
Printed in the United States of America on acid-free paper. ∞

1 2 3 4 5 6 7 8 9 10

The artist used gouache on 140-pound Arches hot-press paper
to create the illustrations for this book.

Permission to use the photograph on page 30
courtesy of the Library of Congress.

For Beth, Sarah, and Lassen —G. H.

For Brenden, Colin, and Scout —A. W.

"Jack here is a fine turkey, isn't he?" said Tad Lincoln.

"I suppose," grumbled the White House gardener.

"He follows me all over the place, now that I've tamed him. Watch."

Tad marched right. The turkey marched right.

Tad marched left. So did the turkey.

"He'll make a tasty dinner, if you ask me," muttered the gardener, bending over to pull a weed.

"No, Jack's not food!" Tad exclaimed.

"He's a pet, just like my goats and rabbits."

"Awaddlewaddlewaddle!" gobbled the turkey.

"Ouch!" hollered the gardener.

"I don't think he likes you much," said Tad.

"Take him away," said the gardener gruffly. "I've got work to do."

Tad led his pet turkey around to the front of the White House.
"You stay here, Jack," he said. "I'll be back to feed you later."

Tad ran up the steps and zipped through the front door, bumping into the butler.

"Oh, it's you," said the butler. "None of your usual mischief today, *please*. We're all busy getting ready for that new holiday your father declared."

"Yes, sir." Tad saluted. "Tomorrow's the first Thanksgiving Day for the whole country."

"Everything must be perfect," said the butler as he rushed away.

Tad squeezed through the line of visitors in the White House corridor.
He looked them over. Most were wounded soldiers, job seekers, and widows
who had lost husbands in the Civil War. For a few hours every afternoon,
Tad's father, Abraham Lincoln, the president of the United States, would
do his best to meet with them.

Tad dashed to the staircase, blocking the path of a young woman with a baby.

"Halt!" Tad ordered in his deepest voice. "Five cents to pass. The proceeds help wounded soldiers in the Union army."

The woman burst into tears.

"What's wrong?" Tad asked, startled.

"Recently I was very ill," she explained, wiping her eyes. "My husband left his army post to come visit me. He went back, but they arrested him for desertion anyway." Her lips trembled. "He's to be shot tomorrow."

Tad winced. "Oh, that's dreadful sad, ma'am."

"I pray the president will pardon him."

"Oh, he will," Tad said, his face brightening. "Pa's a good man."

"There are so many people ahead of me," the woman said anxiously. "I'm afraid I'll be too late."

Suddenly there was a commotion on the stairway above. Tad looked around and noticed one of the president's aides, his mouth tightly drawn, coming down toward him. "Your father wishes to see you," the man said. "Immediately."

Tad turned back to the woman. "What's your name, ma'am?" he asked.

"Elizabeth Miller."

Tad nodded and hurried up the stairs. As he rounded a corner he glanced over his shoulder. The hall was empty. By his father's office, the table with the visitors' calling cards stood unguarded. Tad quickly found Mrs. Miller's and placed it at the top of the pile. Then he knocked on the door.

"Come in," said his father.

Tad found the president writing busily.

"Hello, Tadpole."

"There sure are lots of folks waiting to see you, Pa."

"That's because this war has gone on far too long," his father muttered. "So many killed and wounded."

Tad nodded sadly.

The president removed his spectacles and rubbed his eyes. "Well, at least tomorrow will be a bright spot," he said, motioning for Tad to come closer. "Now, what's this I hear about a toll?"

"It's for wounded soldiers, Pa!"

Mr. Lincoln put a hand on Tad's shoulder. "First you tried to sell our good clothes on the White House lawn. Then you blasted the Cabinet Room door with your toy cannon. And now this toll."

"But, Pa . . ."

His father interrupted. "I think it's fine that you want to raise money to help the soldiers. But charging people to meet with me is not the way. I must be available to the people during these hard times. Do you understand?"

"Yes, Pa," Tad said, looking down.

The president stroked his whiskers. "Why don't you go back to running your fruit stand? That was a good idea, and our visitors appreciated it."

"All right, Pa."

His father winked. "But no more tolls. Now off you go."

Tad opened the door to leave. Outside, next to his father's aide,
stood Mrs. Miller. Tad smiled and went to feed his turkey.

"Here, Jack," he said, pulling some cracked corn out of his pocket. "Pa sure looks worn out sometimes. But tomorrow should do him good. We're going to have a big delicious dinner and everything. I wish you could be there."

"*Awaddlewaddlewaddle!*" gobbled Jack.

Tad laughed. "I've got to find some apples for my fruit stand," he said.

As he turned to go he saw Mrs. Miller coming down the steps.
"God bless your father," she cried. "He pardoned my husband!"

"I told you he would," Tad said.

She wiped away a tear. "Bless you, too."

"You're welcome," Tad said and headed for the kitchen.

When he reached the door, he overheard the cook talking to some servants. "That plump gobbler will make one glorious feast for the president."

Tad crept closer to listen.

"One of you will have to chop off Jack's head," said the cook.

Tad gasped.

He turned and ran along the hallway, then tore upstairs and burst into his father's office. Tears streamed down his cheeks. The president was speaking to one of his advisors and looked around, surprised.

"Pa! Pa!" Tad hollered. "They're going to kill Jack! You can't let them do it, Pa. It would be mean and wicked!"

The president put down his papers. "But, Tad, Jack was sent here to be eaten for our holiday dinner. I thought you knew that."

"No, Pa. I didn't!" Tad wailed. "He's a good turkey, and I don't want him killed. He has as much right to live as anybody. You pardon soldiers all the time, Pa. Can't you pardon Jack?"

Mr. Lincoln sighed, shook his head, and chuckled. He reached for a blank card and repeated aloud as he wrote, "By order of the President of the United States, Jack the turkey is to be spared from execution."

"Perfect, Pa!"

"Here, now. Show this to the cook."

Tad grabbed the card, gave his father a big hug, and fled.

"Then what am I to make for Thanksgiving?" asked the cook,
studying the card Tad had just handed him.

"I don't know," Tad replied happily. "But it won't be Jack!"

The next day, dressed in his best clothes, Tad sat with his mother for Thanksgiving dinner in the White House.

"Before we enjoy this bountiful feast of ham, hen, and vegetables," the president said, rising to speak to the guests, "we should take a moment to remember all those who are helping to hold this country together . . . including fruit-stand vendors."

Tad grinned.

"I think it also fitting," he continued, "being our first national Thanksgiving, that I read from my proclamation, the document that created this holiday."

Tad groaned and wriggled his feet. His mother touched his hand to still him.

President Lincoln adjusted his glasses and began to read:

"I do therefore invite my fellow citizens in every part of the United States, and also those who are at sea and those who are sojourning in foreign lands, to set apart and observe the last Thursday of November as a day of Thanksgiving."

He put down the proclamation and looked around the room.
"Even in times of darkness and despair," he said, "there are still
many things for which to give thanks."

"There sure are!" Tad cried.

The president smiled and sat down. He glanced over at Tad.
"Looks like we'll have a fine Thanksgiving, doesn't it, Tadpole?"

"Yes," said Tad. "And Jack will, too!"

About the Story

Not all the details in this story are true. The times some events occurred have been changed, and the conversations are made up. Most of the things Tad Lincoln did in this story reportedly happened, including saving Jack the turkey and bombarding the Cabinet Room door with his toy cannon. Tad really was determined to raise money to help wounded soldiers and did persuade his father to pardon a woman's husband so he wouldn't be shot. Although Tad's antics often annoyed his father's staff, most agreed he had a big heart and a special way with animals. Once he even hitched goats to a chair and ran them through the White House, upsetting a gathering of dignified ladies. Nothing was too surprising when it came to Tad.

Although several presidents had declared occasional days of thanksgiving, none had ever officially made it a national holiday. Abraham Lincoln finally did so with his Proclamation of Thanksgiving on October 3, 1863.

About the Civil War

The bloodiest war ever fought on United States soil was the Civil War. Brother fought against brother, father against son. The nation had split in two. Eleven states in the South left the Union in 1861 and formed the Confederacy, determined to govern themselves and hold slaves. Abraham Lincoln and the federal government did not agree. On April 12, 1861, Fort Sumter in South Carolina was attacked by Confederate forces. The Civil War had begun. When it finally ended four years later with a Union victory, more than 620,000 men and boys had been killed, and over 50,000 returned home as amputees.

About Abraham Lincoln

Abraham Lincoln was the sixteenth president of the United States. Born in a log cabin near Hodgenville, Kentucky, in 1809, he grew up smart, even though he rarely attended school. While working as a postmaster and surveyor, he began to study law. He married Mary Todd in 1842. Abe eventually entered politics. Shortly after he was elected president in 1861, the Civil War began. Firm in his belief that a divided nation could not survive, Lincoln mobilized the North into action, freed the slaves, and reunified the country. One week after the war ended in April 1865, John Wilkes Booth shot and killed the president at Ford's Theater in Washington, D.C.

Of the Lincolns' four children, only the oldest, Robert, lived to be an adult. Their next two children, Edward and William, died in childhood. Tad, the youngest, was eighteen when he caught a "severe cold," possibly pneumonia, and passed away in 1871.